VIETNAM

REBUILDING A NATION

By Sherry Garland

DILLON PRESS, INC.
Minneapolis, Minnesota 55415

Acknowledgments

My deepest gratitude goes to Terry H. Anderson, associate professor of history at Texas A&M University, and to Rose Eder, head nurse of the children's ward at St. Joseph Hospital in Bryan, Texas, whose recent trip to Vietnam provided most of the photographs used in this book. Special thanks also go out to Vo Khanh, who answered my questions about his native land. And, I especially want to thank my husband, who never complained about my strange hours, moody temperament, and blatant neglect.

Photos are reproduced through the courtesy of Terry Anderson (p. 9, 11, 13, 17, 23, 26, 28, 31, 40, 61, 76, 89, 96, 100, 104, 106); Rose Eder (p. 18); Maurice Durand Collection of Vietnamese Art, Yale University Library (p. 35, 37); the U.S. Department of Defense (p. 49); U.S. Army (p. 53); World Vision International (p. 58, 110); Library of Congress (43); Lien Nga (p. 71); and Rick Graetz (p. 85).

Library of Congress Cataloging-in-Publication Data

Garland, Sherry.
    Vietnam, rebuilding a nation / by Sherry Garland.
      p.   cm. — (Discovering our heritage)
    Includes bibliographical references.
    Summary: Describes the history, people, politics culture, major cities, and other aspects of Vietnam.
    ISBN 0-87518-422-7 (lib. bdg.) : $12.95
     1. Vietnam—Juvenile literature. [1. Vietnam.] I. Title.
  II. Series.
    DS556.3.G37   1990
    959.7—dc20   89-29212
                                           CIP
                                           AC

Dillon Press, Inc., 242 Portland Avenue South
Minneapolis, Minnesota 55415

Printed in the United States of America
1 2 3 4 5 6 7 8 9 10 99 98 97 96 95 94 93 92 91 90

Contents

Fast Facts about Vietnam

Official Name: Socialist Republic of Vietnam.

Capital: Hanoi.

Location: Eastern coast of the Indochinese Peninsula in Southeast Asia. Vietnam is bordered by the People's Republic of China to the north, Laos and Cambodia to the west, and the South China Sea to the east and south.

Area: 127,242 square miles (329,556 square kilometers). *Greatest distances*: north-south—1,030 miles (1,657 kilometers); east-west—380 miles (612 kilometers). At its narrowest point, Vietnam is only 30 miles (48 kilometers) wide. *Coastline:* 2,038 miles (3,280 kilometers).

Elevation: *Highest*—Fan Si Pan peak, at 10,312 feet (3,143 meters) above sea level. *Lowest*—sea level, along the coast.

Population: 62,996,000 (1988 estimate). *Distribution*— 80 percent rural, 20 percent urban. *Density*—495 persons per square mile (191 per square kilometer).

Form of Government: A socialist republic controlled by the Communist party.

Important Products: *Agriculture*—rice, sugarcane, fruit, vegetables, cassava, sweet potatoes, coconuts, maize, fish, pigs, poultry. *Mining*—coal, phosphates, tin, salt. *Industry*—food processing, textiles, fertilizer, lumber, cement, steel.

Basic Unit of Money: Dong.

Major Language: Vietnamese.

Major Religions: Buddhism, Confucianism, Taoism, Roman Catholicism.

Flag: A red field with a gold five-pointed star in the center.

National Anthem: *Tien Quan Ca* ("The Troops Are Advancing").

Major Holidays: New Year's Day—January 1; Tet—January or February (date varies according to lunar calendar); Liberation of Saigon—April 30; May Day—May 1; National Day—September 2-3.

1. Mountains and Rice Paddies

To many Americans, the name "Vietnam" means only one thing—a painful war in the 1960s and 1970s, in which American and South Vietnamese soldiers fought against South Vietnamese rebels and troops from North Vietnam. But the country of Vietnam is more than just its troubled past. It is a beautiful land, with rugged mountains, tumbling rivers, tropical beaches, and lush fields of brilliant green rice. Vietnam has an ancient culture, rich with poets, scholars, artists, legends, and brave heroes. Most importantly, the Vietnamese are hard-working people, determined to survive and re-build their country.

Life in Vietnam is not easy. In the countryside, a farmer might sink knee-deep in the mud behind a water buffalo as he plows his rice field. In one of the nation's crowded cities, an orphan might earn a living by ped-dling cigarettes on a street corner. Vietnam's recovery from its war-torn past has been slow, and today it is one of the poorest nations in the world. Although its large cities have many beautiful buildings built when Viet-nam was a French colony more than fifty years ago, few new buildings have been added since the war ended in 1975. There are few factories or businesses, and most

Vietnamese live in small villages, farming the land and leading much the same life-style as their ancestors.

The *Don Ganh* Country

Vietnam stretches in a long, *S*-shaped curve along the far-eastern coast of the Indochinese Peninsula in Southeast Asia. Its northern neighbor is China, and to the west lie Laos and Cambodia. Splashing against Vietnam's shores on the east and south is the South China Sea. Many miles to the south across this sea are the nations of Malaysia and Indonesia.

Vietnam is a long country, wide at both ends and very narrow in the middle. Although the widest point is almost 400 miles (644 kilometers) across, at its narrowest it is only a 30-mile (48-kilometer) drive from the shore to the border. Because the wide top and bottom of the country contain rich farmlands where nearly all the nation's rice is grown, many Vietnamese like to compare their country to a *don ganh*, a bamboo pole with a basket on each end for carrying rice.

Mountains and hills cover three-fourths of Vietnam's countryside. The main mountain range—the Truong Son, or Annamite, range—runs down the long country like spikes on a dragon's back. The highest peaks rise in the far north, including Fan Si Pan, which at 10,312 feet (3,143 meters) is the highest point in the

The don ganh *can be used to carry produce from the local marketplace.*

country. Some of these mountains even extend into the sea in the north, forming many small, steep islands in Ha Long Bay.

Dense forests or jungles cover much of Vietnam's highlands. More than two hundred rivers flow through the country, often cutting through deep ravines and narrow valleys, creating beautiful, cascading waterfalls. Wild animals such as tigers, panthers, boars, deer, pythons, monkeys, and even herds of elephants roam these jungles. Although many villages dot the hills and mountains, including those of native tribes, only one-fourth of Vietnam's population lives in these highland regions.

With its long coastline of about 2,000 miles (3,220 kilometers), Vietnam has some of the most beautiful beaches in the world. In the north, where mountains extend to the sea, the coast is rugged, with steep lime-stone cliffs. In the south, the beaches are more tropical, with coconut palms waving beside the shiny, white sand.

Fertile River Deltas

Vietnam's wide northern and southern regions each contain an important river delta—a low, flat area cre-ated when a large river splits into smaller branches and flows into the ocean. Nearly three out of every four Vietnamese live in these deltas, even though both deltas together cover only about one-fourth of the country's land. These lowlands are very crowded; in fact, Viet-nam is one of the most crowded nations in the world.

So many of the sixty-two million Vietnamese live in the delta regions because the soil there is very fertile. When the rivers overflow, they deposit minerals and rich earth, called silt, into the surrounding countryside. In Vietnam, the rivers overflow often because the rains

Rice fields cover much of the Vietnamese lowlands.

are very heavy for almost half the year. Farmers can easily grow rice, the nation's main crop and food source.

The Mekong River delta, located in the far south of Vietnam, is the country's largest farming region. One of Asia's longest rivers, the Mekong begins 2,600 miles (4,186 kilometers) away in the mountains of Tibet, tumbling through the rugged highlands of China, Laos, Thailand, and Cambodia before arriving in Vietnam, where it empties into the South China Sea. In northern

Vietnam, the Song Ka—or Red River—delta earned its name because the water often appears red in color.

Vietnam's largest city, Ho Chi Minh City, is located near the edge of the Mekong delta. With a population of almost four million, Ho Chi Minh City is very crowded. Its streets are lined with beautiful buildings, majestic churches, and grand hotels, built by the French many years ago. Today, most of the buildings are rundown, and many residents cannot find jobs. Those who do, often work for the government or for plants that process foods such as sugar, tea, coffee, fruit, and tobacco.

The capital of Vietnam—and its second largest city—is Hanoi, located in the Red River delta. As in all large Vietnamese cities, bicycles and motorbikes fill the streets, but there are few cars. In the north, coal and other minerals are mined, and factories manufacture fertilizer and forests products. Haiphong, the nation's largest seaport, is nearby on the Gulf of Tonkin.

Central Vietnam

The Ben Hai River flows across Vietnam near its narrowest point. From 1954 to 1975, this river served as the line that divided Vietnam into two separate countries. Today, it is just another beautiful river winding through the mountains. About 100 miles (161 kilo-

The influence of French rulers can be seen in the style of many buildings in Ho Chi Minh City.

meters) south, on the River of Perfumes, lies the city of Hue, which once served as the capital of a Vietnamese empire. As a former home to emperors, Hue has many royal tombs, majestic palaces, and colorful pagodas. The years of war destroyed many of these buildings, but the Vietnamese are working to restore them.

About fifty miles (eighty kilometers) south of Hue is Da Nang, the site of an important military base during the 1960s. Today, all that remains of the base are deserted watchtowers and pieces of scrap metal, which the residents gather and sell. Farther inland lies a region called the Central Highlands. Here, the rolling hills and windswept plains receive less rainfall than any other area of Vietnam.

All along the coast, fishermen gather their catch from the South China Sea. Fish is a favorite dish of many Vietnamese, but they often do not get to eat as much fish as they would like. Vietnam lost many of its fishing boats because they were used by people trying to flee the country after the war was over.

Monsoons and Rice Farming

Vietnam's climate is semitropical, and the weather remains hot most of the year. Around May, winds called monsoons blow across the country from the seas to the southwest. Where these moist winds hit the

Indochina Peninsula, rain begins to pour. The rivers overflow and city streets and rice fields flood.

In October, the monsoon winds switch directions. They blow from the northeast, over land, and no longer bring heavy rains. These winds leave the land dry and cause the water level of the rivers to fall.

During the seasons when the monsoons are switching directions, the weather is often violent. Severe storms with strong winds and pounding rains hit the coastal towns. Called typhoons, these storms are similar to the hurricanes that strike American coasts.

Monsoon rains may seem inconvenient, but Vietnamese farmers depend on them for the survival of their crops. Young rice plants must be grown in flooded fields, called paddies. If the rains come too late, the young plants will not grow strong and healthy.

Nearly three out of every four Vietnamese are farmers and live in small villages. Many farmers work on government-owned collectives, where all work together to grow the crops. In other areas, people farm on their own individual plots of land, but they must still give part of their crops to the government.

Many village houses are made of heavy bamboo. Houses near the water are usually built on stilts, raised several feet off the ground to protect them from the frequent floods. In highland areas, some houses have deep trenches around them to keep out wild animals.

Besides rice, Vietnamese farmers grow crops such as sweet potatoes, vegetables, melons, bananas, oranges, beans, sorghum, and maize. On large plantations that were originally built by the French, they raise rubber trees, sugarcane, cotton, tobacco, and tea.

The Mountain People

In the Vietnamese highlands, the air is full of the sound of chattering monkeys and colorful, screaming birds. The dark-skinned people living in these mountainous areas are the descendants of the first people to inhabit Vietnam thousands of years ago. The lighter-skinned ethnic Vietnamese at one time called these mountain villagers *moi*, which means "savages." Today, they are called Montagnards, which comes from the French word meaning "mountain people."

There are thirty-four Montagnard tribes spread over Vietnam, each with its own language, customs, beliefs, and leaders. Many of them farm, and the men hunt in the jungles, using bows and arrows to kill deer and game birds. The mountain people respect nature and are sometimes very brave—a man may face a tiger alone, with only a knife for protection!

Most Montagnards live in long, narrow huts raised on stilts to keep out tigers, boars, and large snakes. Many relatives live inside, often adding up to thirty

A hut in the Vietnamese highlands.

people. Men often wear shorts, and some wrap colorful turbans around their heads. Most tribal women wear long, wrap-around skirts and carry their babies in cloth pouches strapped to their backs.

When traveling through the jungle, Montagnards carry machetes—a type of knife with a heavy blade—to chop through the dense plants, because footpaths do not last long. In lowlands, tall "elephant grass" grows. Its sharp edges can slice the bare arms and legs.

A Montagnard woman carries her young child in a sling on her back.

A Struggling Nation

Vietnam is governed by a National Assembly, whose 496 members are elected by voters every five years. The assembly members, in turn, elect a smaller Council of State, which functions as Vietnam's ruling body. Each village, town, and district elects its own leaders, who serve on People's Councils. Although the Vietnamese vote for their government members, only one political party is allowed, the Communist party. The country's laws reflect the Communist belief that all property should be owned by the government.

Today, the Vietnamese people are very poor—most city dwellers cannot find jobs, and severe inflation has caused many goods, such as clothing, bicycles, and school supplies, to cost more than most people can afford. Medicine is very expensive, and many people cannot afford to buy it when they get sick.

Although Vietnam is rich in many natural resources, it lacks factories and industry. The country has the world's largest anthracite coal mines, as well as phosphates, tin, zinc, lead, manganese, gold, and off-shore oil. Its many rivers could provide water power for electricity, and its forests contain valuable hardwoods, such as teak. Unfortunately, the government does not have the funds available to build the plants needed to process these resources.

The Vietnamese people have suffered many hardships in the past fifty years, including war, floods, drought, and crop failures. They are determined to rebuild their nation, though, and are proud of the ancient heritage shared by all Vietnamese—north and south.

2. Children of the Dragon

In their legends, the Vietnamese claim to be the descendants of a dragon. About four thousand years ago, they say, a brave dragon prince named Lac-Long-Quan married a beautiful fairy named Au-Co and had one hundred children. Half lived with their mother in the mountains, and half moved with their father near the sea. There, the oldest son founded the first Vietnamese empire. Even today, Vietnamese poets proudly call their people the "grandchildren of Lac."

The dragon is the most admired of the twelve signs in the Chinese zodiac, which is popular in Vietnam. Many people believe that the zodiac uses the stars and planets to read the future or a person's character. The Chinese zodiac has a different sign every year, repeating after twelve years. For example, 1988 was the Year of the Dragon. People born under the sign of the dragon are said to be energetic, capable, sensitive, brave, and devoted, often to the point of being stubborn.

These "dragon" traits have carried the Vietnamese people through many troubled times in their past. They showed their bravery and devotion during the war, and today they tackle the problems of rebuilding their land with energy.

A Blending of Cultures

Over the past four thousand years, many invaders came to Vietnam, each bringing its own culture. The Vietnamese learned to adapt to foreign cultures, absorbing parts until they all blended together into a uniquely Vietnamese way of life.

Many invaders brought their own religious beliefs. Buddhism—brought by the Indians and Chinese—is the main religion of Vietnam today. Buddhists believe that humans suffer because they desire worldly possessions and pleasures, and they try to overcome this by living a life devoted to patience and goodness. Buddhist temples and shrines dot the countryside and cities. Worshipers light incense and bring offerings of fruit or flowers to express their devotion. Many homes and businesses also have small Buddhist altars.

From Confucius, a famous Chinese teacher, the Vietnamese learned the need for strict social and family order, and a great respect for ancestors and authority figures such as the emperor, teachers, and fathers. Today, nearly every Vietnamese home has pictures of beloved relatives on a shelf or home altar. Families hold celebrations to mark the anniversary of the death of respected ancestors. People pray to the ancestors' spirits for guidance and to protect their family.

Some Vietnamese are Taoists. They believe in

many gods and practice harmony between humans and nature. Many Montagnards also practice animism, the belief that animals, trees, and even rocks and streams have spirits. They pray to these spirits and watch for omens from nature.

The French, who did much to change the course of Vietnamese history, brought the Roman Catholic religion with them. Although many Vietnamese Catholics fled the country when the Communists took control in 1975, the beautiful churches built by the French remain. Today, about 14 percent of the Vietnamese people practice the Catholic religion.

Many Vietnamese combine the practices of different religions in their everyday lives. A family may pray to its ancestors, maintain an altar, and believe in the zodiac, fortune tellers, and omens. People may try to improve their luck by following traditional beliefs— much as some Americans carry a rabbit's foot for luck.

Duty to Family

The family is the center of Vietnamese life, the place where beliefs and customs are passed down from one generation to the next. Vietnamese families are very large and close-knit. As many members as possible live in the same house—grandparents, parents, children, and sometimes even aunts, uncles, and cousins.

Older people are important members of Vietnamese society, and are treated with great respect.

With such large families, order and rules are needed to keep things running smoothly. Everyone has a role to play and must contribute to the family's well-being and honor. Family members try to avoid fighting or any action that might bring shame, such as being expelled from school or breaking the law. Young people must respect older family members, serve them first at meals, and ask them for advice. The Vietnamese believe that the older a person becomes, the wiser he or she gets. When the parents grow very old, the adult children will take care of them, to repay them for being born and raised.

Sacrifice and loyalty to family is a Vietnamese tradition. Most parents help their children obtain a good education, even if it means going without possessions themselves. Brothers and sisters may sacrifice for the family, too. A Vietnamese boy may get a job to help pay for his brother's schooling, knowing that his brother will help him later. A girl may cancel her wedding or quit school to take care of a sick mother and help raise her younger brothers and sisters. Because families are so close, rural Vietnamese young people rarely move far away from the village where they were born.

Politeness and good manners are as important in the family as they are in Vietnamese society. Children are expected to be patient and not interrupt while adults are talking. Visitors are treated courteously, and given food and drink when they enter a home. Most Vietnamese do not like to criticize family or friends in public. They try to avoid displeasing anyone, and may even tell a "little white lie" to avoid hurting another person's feelings.

Friends are valued as much as family. People try to help their friends in time of trouble, often by loaning possessions or money. Vietnamese are willing to aid a friend in need because they know that someday they may need help, too. Helping each other is important in a country where few can afford to pay for services.

The Vietnamese express many of these values in their poetry, which is the nation's most popular form of literature. In ancient Vietnam, all educated men were also poets. During wars, soldiers often wrote poems before battle, or quoted lines from well-known poems. Even today, many Vietnamese can quote several lines from *Kim Van Kieu*, the nation's most famous poem, which is about love and sacrifice.

The Life of a Farmer

Because most Vietnamese are farmers, their daily lives follow the rhythm of the planting and harvesting of rice. The life of a rice farmer is very hard. Before anything can be planted, he must plow the muddy fields

with the help of a water buffalo. The farmer works long hours, with little chance for rest, to prepare the fields for the monsoon rains.

When the water buffalo, or *con trau*, is not plowing fields or hauling heavy loads, it loves to soak in a pool of muddy water, with nothing but its head sticking out. The boys who take care of these large, ox-like animals are called *chan trau*, or "buffalo boys." They ride on the animals' backs, often singing songs to them.

About a month before planting time, farmers scatter rice seeds in flooded paddies surrounded by small clay or dirt walls called dikes. Millions of tiny rice seedlings, called *ma*, shoot up. The farmers pull up handfuls of the seedlings, tie them in bundles, and carry them to larger paddies. Then, they separate each seedling and press it into the soggy ground, making neat rows. The farmers do all this work by hand, and the constant stooping makes their backs ache.

Once the plants are growing, the farmers pull weeds and keep water in the paddies by dipping straw buckets into irrigation ditches and hoisting the water into the rice fields. To protect themselves from the hot sun or rain, the farmers wear cone-shaped straw hats called *non la*.

When the rice plants are ripe, the farmers harvest the yellow stalks with a sharp, curved knife called a *cai liem*. To separate the grain from the stalks, women beat

A chan trau *and his water buffalo.*

Some farmers lay their rice on busy roadways to speed threshing.

them against bamboo poles and then pound the grain in big baskets to loosen the outer hulls. Farmers who live along highways often lay their rice out on the road, so that passing vehicles will run over it, and speed the threshing process. In the final step—called winnowing—women toss baskets of threshed rice into the air, where the wind blows away the lighter hulls, leaving the rice kernels behind.

Life in the Capital

Although farmers in Vietnam live in much the same way throughout the country, people in northern cities may have different life-styles from those in southern cities. Differences in the two region's governments and cultures during the war still influence the way people live today.

Northern Vietnam has had a strict Communist government for almost thirty-five years, and Hanoi, the capital, is the home of many high-ranking government officials. Life in the city can be hard. The government has placed loudspeakers on street corners and buildings throughout the city. Early in the morning, people wake up to the sound of music and announcements. By 6:00 A.M., parks in town fill up with citizens doing morning exercises such as running, badminton, soccer, and *tai chi chuan*, a type of slow-moving martial art.

Parts of Hanoi look like a French country town, with pink stucco houses with green shutters. Yet most buildings are run-down, and if they need repair, there are no paint, plaster, nails, or other materials available to fix them. To save power, the government turns off the electricity from sunrise to sunset, so daytime cooking is done mostly with wood or coal. At night, residents who don't have electricity may use lanterns or candles for light. Televisions are rare, and most programs are imported from the Soviet Union.

Many ordinary items are scarce in Hanoi. Residents recycle everything they can, cleverly turning it into something else. When clothing, cooking utensils, and other everyday products are available, they can be very expensive. A modest meal at a restaurant, for example, might cost a month's salary! Money is so scarce that many people use cigarettes instead of the Vietnamese unit of money, the *dong*.

Vietnamese have to be very careful about what they say in public because they are not allowed to criticize the government openly. Lawbreakers may be sent to the "Hanoi Hilton," a famous prison where American prisoners of war were once held.

Ho Chi Minh City

Southern Vietnam's largest city, Ho Chi Minh City, has more of an international flavor than Hanoi. Once called Saigon, it was the center of French colonial trade in Southeast Asia. Even today, people sip French iced coffee in little sidewalk cafes or buy bread from French bakeries. Many older residents still speak the French language. Although the Americans were not in Vietnam as long as the French, many teenagers' favorite music is American rock'n'roll. They dress in American-style clothes and watch American movies.

Even in the cities, many tasks are still done the traditional way, such as milling lumber by hand.

Ho Chi Minh City bustles with people on bicycles, motorbikes, and a few cars and buses. Instead of taxis, Vietnamese ride in *cyclos*, three-wheeled bikes with a passenger seat in the front. Shops sell radios, clothing, produce, and even monkeys and snakes! The sidewalks are crowded with small businesses such as bicycle and shoe repair shops.

In Ho Chi Minh City, men may wear European-style shirts and pants, and many young people wear

T-shirts with American slogans. Women usually wear pants and blouses, but for special occasions they may dress in a traditional *ao dai*. This is a long-sleeved, high-necked garment, split up the sides and flowing gracefully below the knees over loose, billowy pants.

One famous part of Ho Chi Minh City is called Cholon. It is the traditional home to the city's large Chinese population. These Chinese follow their own customs, speak their own language, attend their own schools and temples, and rarely marry Vietnamese.

A sad reminder of the presence of Americans in Vietnam is Ho Chi Minh City's many Amerasians, the children of American servicemen and Vietnamese women. Because these children are considered shameful to their families, they and their mothers are forced to live on their own and support themselves as best they can. Without the aid of their families, life is harsh for the Amerasians. Today, they are teenagers or young adults, and they often must live on the streets.

The unfortunate fate of the Amerasians shows how important families are in Vietnam. The country is so poor that family members must help each other survive, often working at several jobs to earn money. Families are ready to sacrifice for each other, to help the family as a whole. This ability to adapt and survive is important for the children of the dragon.

3. A Land of Empires

The first people to live where Vietnam is today were tribes of the last Ice Age. Hunters and gatherers, they belonged to the same race of people as those living today in Malaysia, Indonesia, and the Philippines.

A more advanced civilization called the Viets developed later in what is now southern China. The Viets were not Chinese—they had a different culture and language from the Chinese. After a time, the Viets began moving south to get away from Chinese invasions. They settled in the area that is northern Vietnam today. In 208 B.C., several Viet groups united, to form a kingdom called Nam Viet. The word *nam* means "south," so the name of this new kingdom meant Southern Viets.

As the Viets moved south, they fought with the native tribes, driving many into the mountains. They married others, and the mixture of these two groups formed the ethnic Vietnamese race that now accounts for about 85 percent of all people in Vietnam.

In Viet society, most of the land belonged to a few wealthy, powerful landowners. Peasants grew the crops and gave most of their produce to the landlords, in exchange for the right to live on the land. This way of life continued for much of Vietnam's history.

Under Chinese Rule

The kingdom of Nam Viet did not remain independent for long. By 111 B.C., the Chinese had conquered the country, beginning a rule that lasted almost one thousand years. It influenced the culture of Vietnam more than any other foreign rule.

The Chinese brought farming improvements, the Buddhist religion, a writing system, and a form of village government to Vietnam. The Vietnamese accepted these improvements—upper-class citizens were soon dressing, eating, speaking, reading, and writing like the Chinese. Secretly, though, the Vietnamese resented being ruled by the Chinese. In A.D. 39, two sisters—Trung Trac and Trung Nhi—led the first successful revolt. When the Chinese finally overthrew them, the sisters threw themselves into a river rather than surrender.

Another woman led a rebellion about two hundred years later. Trieu Au was only twenty-three years old. Dressed in golden armor and riding an elephant, she led a thousand soldiers into battle. After being defeated, she, too, killed herself rather than surrender.

The Vietnamese did not give up the idea of being independent. Ly Bon led another unsuccessful rebellion in 543, but he developed a method of fighting that has been used successfully throughout Vietnam's history. In guerrilla warfare, soldiers engage in surprise attacks

Trieu Au and her elephant ride into battle.

and hit-and-run fighting. Because they are usually out-numbered, they must depend on not being seen by their enemy.

The Vietnamese Empire

In 938, General Ngo Quyen led the Vietnamese to independence by defeating the Chinese at the battle of Bach Dang River. In this battle, the Vietnamese drove iron spikes into the riverbed below the surface of the water. The Chinese fleet sailed into the spikes without seeing them and were attacked by the Vietnamese forces. The country remained independent for most of the next nine hundred years under the name *Dai Viet*, which means "Greater Viet."

Several dynasties, or ruling families, governed Vietnam during this period, using the form of government established by the Chinese. The emperor was head of the empire. He was advised and served by mandarins—officials who were chosen by passing very difficult exams.

As the population of Dai Viet grew, settlers began moving farther south because they needed more farmland. As they journeyed, they discovered other kingdoms, which they fought to take their land. This policy was called *nam tien*, which means "marching south."

One of these kingdoms was Champa, which had been founded by the descendants of seafaring Indian merchants. For four hundred years, the Vietnamese and Chams fought viciously. Today, all that remains of the once-great kingdom of Champa are majestic ruins and a few Chams living in Vietnam's highlands. The Vietnamese also conquered the ancient kingdom of the Khmers, or Cambodians, to obtain the rich Mekong delta.

In the thirteenth century, the Mongol emperor

General Tran Hung Dao was a master of guerrilla warfare.

Kublai Khan attacked Dai Viet. Khan's great army out-numbered the Vietnamese more than two to one, but the Vietnamese general was a master of guerrilla warfare. Vietnam became one of the few countries in the world to drive off the famous Mongol invaders.

By 1407, Dai Viet was weak from fighting, and the Chinese conquered the Vietnamese again. This time the Chinese ruled harshly, outlawing Vietnamese customs and profiting from its natural resources. A leader named Le Loi defeated the Chinese in 1428 and became the emperor. Considered Vietnam's greatest emperor because of his land reforms and code of justice, Le Loi founded the Le dynasty, one of the country's longest.

Over the next two hundred years, the Le dynasty slowly lost power. A civil war raged between two powerful landowning families, the Nguyens in the south and the Trinhs in the north. In 1673, they agreed to a truce and divided Dai Viet into two separate countries. Vietnam was reunited again about a hundred years later, following a rebellion led by three brothers from the Tay Son region.

The Arrival of the Europeans

While the Vietnamese were fighting their civil wars, European nations began sending traders to Southeast Asia, looking for valuable spices. In 1637, the Portuguese built the first European trading port in Vietnam, but they soon abandoned it. Other European countries also tried and failed to develop trade with Vietnam— the Vietnamese distrusted foreigners and did not wish to trade with them. After a few years, the only Europeans left in Vietnam were missionaries.

Brought by the Portuguese, Roman Catholic missionaries converted thousands of Vietnamese. Yet the emperors did not like Christianity because they considered themselves the nation's religious leaders. They began to persecute Catholic priests and newly converted Vietnamese Christians.

One French missionary, Alexandre de Rhodes, believed that Vietnam should become a French colony, and he tried to convince the government in France of Vietnam's great wealth. De Rhodes also perfected the system of writing Vietnamese that is still used today. Called *quoc ngu*, this system uses the Roman alphabet and accent marks instead of the Chinese characters that had been used.

The French increased their influence in Vietnam by supporting a young heir to the throne, Nguyen Anh, who became emperor in 1802. Nguyen Anh moved the capital to Hue and renamed the country Viet Nam. Hue became the cultural center of Vietnam, attracting many artists, poets, and musicians. The Nguyen dynasty would rule the last great empire in Vietnam.

Under French Rule

By the mid-nineteenth century, the French government wanted to take control of Vietnam with its abundance of rich farmland, mineral deposits, and cheap labor. Claiming that it was protecting Catholic missionaries, France sent soldiers to capture Da Nang in 1858 and Saigon in 1861. Within twenty years, the

This ruin is a reminder of Hue's former status as a national capital and cultural center.

north fell, and all of Vietnam was under French rule. The country's nine hundred years of independence had ended.

One of the first things the French did to discourage Vietnamese unity was to stop using the name *Vietnam*. They divided the country into three parts: Tonkin in the north, Annam in the center, and Cochin China in the south. The emperor was allowed to remain in Annam, but he had little power. French power and culture grew strongest in the south, especially in Saigon, its capital.

The French built roads, railroads, hospitals, and schools. In the north, they set up industries, such as coal mining. In the south, they established large plantations of rubber, tea, coffee, tobacco, and cotton. These businesses were very profitable, but most Vietnamese were not allowed to share the profits. The French and Chinese merchants owned 95 percent of the businesses in Vietnam.

As the population grew and more land was converted into large plantations, many peasants were left without land to farm. Some moved to large cities and worked under harsh conditions in factories, often having no homes to live in. Others worked in mines or on plantations for low wages. Although more Vietnamese were becoming educated, French law did not allow Vietnamese to hold public office or positions of importance. By the early twentieth century, the Vietnamese were growing unhappy with their French rulers. They began forming nationalist groups to work for independence.

The Nationalist Movement

One young nationalist, who called himself Ho Chi Minh, was well-educated, spoke several languages, and traveled to many countries. In England, he worked as a dishwasher; in Paris, he was a photographer's assistant.

Ho Chi Minh greatly admired the American Revolution and especially the American Declaration of Independence. He felt Americans would understand Vietnam's great desire to be free of its French colonial rulers.

Unfortunately, the U.S. government ignored his ideas, and Ho soon became a Communist. For thirty years, Ho Chi Minh traveled, studying in China and the Soviet Union, using many names, and living in small, run-down quarters. Always his goal was to seek support for his idea of a free Vietnam.

During the worldwide Great Depression of the 1930s, communism grew in popularity among the starving Vietnamese peasants. The French government tried to shut down these groups by arresting suspected Communists and bombing villages.

In the late 1930s, World War II began. Japan emerged as a powerful Asian nation, conquering many of its neighbors, including Vietnam. Many other Southeast Asians praised Japan as a liberator, but Ho Chi Minh distrusted the Japanese. In 1941, he returned to his homeland for the first time in thirty years. He united Communist and non-Communist nationalist groups to form the *Viet Nam Doc Lap Dong Minh* (Vietnam Independence League), or *Vietminh* for short. This group wanted to remove all foreigners from Vietnam, both Japanese and French.

Ho Chi Minh (left) *meets China's Chairman Mao during his travels through Asia.*

While the Japanese occupied Vietnam, Ho Chi Minh and his Vietminh band lived in the rugged northern mountains, where General Vo Nguyen Giap trained the rebels in guerrilla warfare. The U.S. government sent OSS officers—forerunners of the modern CIA—to help train the Vietminh to fight the Japanese. Soon, the Vietminh gained support in the villages.

In 1945, the Japanese surrendered to the Americans, leaving Vietnam without an official government. The Vietminh quickly seized control of towns and villages across the country, sometimes peacefully, sometimes more violently. On September 2, in front of a crowd of thousands in Hanoi, Ho Chi Minh declared Vietnam to be free and independent. He called this new nation the Democratic Republic of Vietnam. The reading of his Declaration of Independence marked the beginning of one of the stormiest periods in Vietnam's history.

4. *The Long Struggle*

Ho Chi Minh patterned the Vietnamese Declaration of Independence after that of the United States because he hoped to gain American approval of his new country. Many Vietnamese, both Communists and non-Communists, supported the new state. Even the emperor, Bao Dai, gave up his throne to show his support for independence.

The French Indochinese War

Vietnam's dreams for independence did not last long, though. Other nations—including Great Britain, the United States, the Soviet Union, and China—did not recognize Ho Chi Minh's government, and the French were not ready to give up their wealthy colony so easily. Within only a few weeks, French troops had reconquered all of southern Vietnam.

Although the French were able to re-establish control, they could not put down the resistance. In a fateful speech, Ho Chi Minh warned the French leaders: "If we must fight, then fight we will. You will kill ten of our men when we kill only one of yours. But, even so, it is you who will finally give up." In December 1946,

Vietminh guerrillas attacked French troops in Hanoi, beginning the war in earnest.

Nearly everyone thought the French would win easily because they had better weapons and highly trained soldiers. Yet the Vietnamese were determined to win their independence, no matter how long it took or what price they had to pay. Their motto became, "Nothing is more important than freedom."

In 1949, the French created the State of Vietnam, persuading Bao Dai to return to the throne. On paper, this new Vietnam was independent, but in reality Bao Dai's government was controlled by the French. Although most Vietnamese supported the struggle for independence, the United States formally recognized the State of Vietnam and began sending aid to help the French fight the Vietminh.

The war dragged on for years, with neither side winning. Finally in 1954, a terrible battle brought the war to an end. The French had built a large fortress in a valley called Dien Bien Phu, in northern Vietnam. This camp became crowded with soldiers, tanks, and heavy artillery, and was supplied both by roads and an airport. The French felt certain that the Vietminh could not move heavy artillery into the rugged hills surrounding the valley.

Although the Vietminh had no trucks or other vehicles for moving heavy equipment, they did have bicycles, determination, and the support of the peasants. By reinforcing their sturdy bicycles to carry more than four hundred pounds (182 kilograms), and by wrapping their clothes around the wheels to silence the noise, the Vietnamese were able to carry guns and heavy artillery hundreds of miles from China to the hills around Dien Bien Phu—sometimes one piece at a time. They moved silently, day and night, bending tree branches over the narrow path to hide their movements from airplanes overhead. Finally, about 50,000 Vietminh soldiers and cannons were hidden in the hills above the French fortress.

The Vietminh took the French by surprise, quickly destroying the airport and supply roads. In the fortress, the soldiers slowly ran out of ammunition, medicine, and food. Although the French fought bravely, after fifty-six days they finally had to surrender. Ho Chi Minh's prediction had come true.

The Two Vietnams

After the battle of Dien Bien Phu, the French knew it was hopeless to continue fighting. In July 1954, France and Vietnam signed a peace agreement in Geneva, Switzerland, in a conference also attended by the United States, Great Britain, China, the Soviet Union, Laos, and Cambodia. According to this agreement,

Vietnam was to be temporarily divided in half. Ho Chi
Minh would be leader of North Vietnam, and South
Vietnam would be governed by Bao Dai and Ngo Dinh
Diem. There were to be elections in two years, to re-
unite the country under one government.

From the beginning, there were problems in both
North and South Vietnam. In the north, the new Communist government took control of all businesses,
seized land from the landowners and gave it to the
peasants, and jailed or killed people who opposed the
changes. Fearing the Communists, hundreds of thousands of northern Catholics moved south.

In the south, Diem—a devoted Catholic—began
persecuting Buddhists and other non-Catholics. His government was also corrupt. Diem's family members and
advisers stole money and killed or jailed opponents.
Fighting occurred daily in the streets of Saigon. In
1955, emperor Bao Dai lost what little power he had
and moved to France. Diem became president of the
nation, called the Republic of Vietnam.

Most of the Vietminh in South Vietnam had
moved to the north, but those who remained put up
posters and campaigned to gather support for Ho Chi
Minh in the elections that were supposed to happen in
1956. Diem began calling these people *Viet Cong*,
which means "Vietnamese Communists," even though
many of them were not Communists at all.

An aerial view of the Ho Chi Minh Trail after it was widened.

The War Begins

By late 1957, the elections had not been held because the governments in North and South Vietnam could not agree on how to hold them. In protest, Viet Cong guerrillas began raiding villages throughout the south and blowing up buildings in Saigon. Within a year, North Vietnam was openly supporting these rebels. They sent soldiers and supplies south down the Ho Chi Minh Trail, an ancient trail that wove through

Laos and Cambodia into a part of South Vietnam called the Central Highlands.

The Ho Chi Minh Trail was dangerous and narrow in places. Soldiers had to travel it by foot, crossing mountain rivers and cutting through dense forests. They were often attacked by mosquitoes or leeches, and many died from diseases. Later, as the war progressed, the trail was widened to allow travel by military vehicles.

More and more South Vietnamese were becoming dissatisfied with Diem's corrupt government. Both Communist and non-Communist groups that opposed Diem united to form the National Liberation Front, a rebel group which openly fought the government. Buddhists began publicly protesting Diem's policies, sometimes setting themselves on fire. Finally in 1963, Diem and his brother were assassinated in a military coup.

The United States Steps In

After Diem's assassination, the government of South Vietnam went through a troubled period. One leader after another was quickly overthrown. The U.S. government had been sending money, weapons, and advisers to aid the South Vietnamese government since the early 1950s, but now the aid increased dramatically. In a little more than a year, the number of American advisers in South Vietnam went from about 700 to more than 15,000.

At first, the advisers were not allowed to fight, but this situation changed quickly. In August 1964, the U.S. government announced that two American ships had been attacked in the Gulf of Tonkin, off the North Vietnamese coast. U.S. planes began bombing North Vietnam, and the first American combat troops landed on the beach at Da Nang in March 1965. Other nations began sending troops also, including Australia, New Zealand, South Korea, Thailand, and the Philippines.

The United States had been victorious in past wars because it had powerful modern weapons—aircraft, tanks, bombs, guns, and ships—as well as well-trained soldiers. The American forces developed a strategy based on the idea that the army with the most power would eventually win. Besides bombing North Vietnam, they used a tactic called "search and destroy" in the South Vietnamese countryside. In this tactic, soldiers uncovered Viet Cong hideouts and then radioed for airplanes to bomb the sites, destroying them.

The Viet Cong and North Vietnamese were fighting a different kind of war, using guerrilla tactics as their ancestors had. They avoided large-scale battles, which they knew the Americans would win. Instead, guerrillas attacked small groups of soldiers, often at night, or lured the soldiers into jungle areas filled with mines and homemade booby-traps. They created weapons out of innocent-looking materials, such as bits of glass and nails inside an exploding mudball.

The guerrillas used their knowledge of Vietnam's jungles, mountains, and rice paddies to build hideouts that were almost impossible to find. In some areas, they built underground tunnels that were large enough to house entire families, schools, and hospitals. Yet the guerrillas' biggest advantage was that they were Vietnamese people fighting on Vietnamese soil. They were used to the extreme heat, insects, monsoon rains, and diseases. They could communicate with the people easily and often dressed like villagers. Many times, Americans could not tell the Viet Cong from the innocent bystanders. Sometimes, women and even children aided the guerrilla soldiers in their fighting.

Villages at War

A famous Vietnamese general once said, "Whoever wins the hearts of the peasants will win the war." Although he was speaking of a war waged hundreds of years ago, his words have remained true throughout Vietnamese history. Both the Americans and the Viet Cong tried to win the support of the South Vietnamese villagers, but in different ways.

One young man, Trung, remembers how the Viet

A United States Ranger gives medical aid to a Vietnamese villager.

Cong persuaded his village to support them. One day, a group of Viet Cong visited the village, taking food and several young men—including Trung's older brother—away. Later, American and South Vietnamese soldiers came to the village and questioned people about the Viet Cong. Some of the people wanted to help, but they were afraid that if they said anything, their sons would be killed. One man spoke up, and the next time the Viet Cong came to the village, he was shot.

The Americans tried to win the hearts of the villagers by giving them clothing and medical care, but at the same time some of their battle tactics created ill feelings. In their search and destroy missions, U.S. soldiers sometimes destroyed whole villages, where families had lived for generations. In one operation, the Americans took villagers to a refugee camp. The soldiers then burned the villagers' orchards and crops, and used bulldozers to flatten their homes. Although this operation uncovered a Viet Cong hideout with tunnels and supplies, the Viet Cong soldiers themselves had fled. More importantly, the anger and resentment felt by the villagers could not be undone by the American soldiers.

South Vietnamese villagers were hurt the most by the war. American napalm bombs destroyed their homes and crops, deadly chemicals such as Agent Orange killed their trees, and the Viet Cong took their food. The Viet Cong killed people they believed helped the Americans, and the Americans killed people they believed helped the Viet Cong. Millions of villagers fled the countryside, moving to cities such as Saigon, where they lived as refugees with no jobs or money.

Yet the North Vietnamese also suffered because American planes bombed northern industries, seaports, and roads in an effort to stop weapons and supplies from being manufactured and sent to the south. To protect themselves from the bombing, the North Vietnamese dug special shelters and wore helmets. Families, factory workers, and schools scheduled their daily activities around the times the bombs were expected. Children learned to run for shelters whenever they heard the warning sirens.

The War Ends

In 1968, one of the most important battles of the war took place. The Tet Offensive earned its name because it started during the celebration of Tet, the Vietnamese new year's festival. Both sides had agreed to stop fighting during the holiday, but the North Vietnamese and Viet Cong launched surprise attacks across South Vietnam, fighting openly for the first time. Some of the bitterest fighting occurred in Hue, where Viet Cong soldiers massacred about three thousand people.

In the United States, protests against the war increased as people watched scenes of the battles on the evening news. Peace talks were opened in Paris, and the United States began slowly withdrawing its troops. Yet the fighting soon expanded into nearby Laos and Cambodia. American planes bombed these neutral countries, attempting to destroy the Ho Chi Minh Trail.

The fighting in South Vietnam and bombing of North Vietnam continued until January 1973, when both sides signed a cease-fire agreement. In March of that year, the last American troops left the country.

The fighting soon started again. Early in 1975, North Vietnamese and Viet Cong troops invaded the Central Highlands. People jammed the roads leading to the sea, hoping to escape farther south by boat. Thousands of people died in this journey, called the "Convoy of Tears." Soon Hue and Da Nang were captured, and another million people fled south or tried to escape on boats. Many people were killed in the crush to board planes and ships. As North Vietnamese troops drew near to Saigon, people panicked. Helicopters rescued thousands of American civilians and South Vietnamese officials while rockets bombed the airport.

On April 30, 1975, North Vietnamese tanks rumbled down the deserted streets of Saigon. People who had not been able to leave hid in their houses, afraid that the Communists would murder them. A tank burst through the gates of the presidential palace. A soldier raised the Viet Cong flag over the building, and the war was finally over.

The New Nation

About two million Vietnamese had died during the war, four million were wounded, and six million were left homeless. Another one million Vietnamese had fled to other nations. Buildings, factories, businesses, farms, and jungles had been destroyed.

The united country was renamed the Socialist Republic of Vietnam. The new Communist government took control of South Vietnam's businesses, killing or jailing people who opposed it. Thousands of people were moved from cities to rural areas and forced to build farms. Many of these people died from their harsh new life. Others were sent to special "re-education" camps. There, they were treated as prisoners, tortured, and forced to learn Communist beliefs.

In 1978, fighting broke out between Vietnam and Cambodia. Vietnamese soldiers drove Cambodia's Communist leaders from its capital and set up a new Communist government there. This action angered many nations. China briefly invaded Vietnam's northern border. The United States and some other Western nations cut all ties with Vietnam. This left Vietnam isolated, and it grew to depend on the Soviet Union for aid.

As tension increased with China, the Vietnamese government forced hundreds of thousands of its Chinese residents to leave Vietnam. Many ethnic Vietnamese fled with them. Because many of these new refugees left by boat, they have been called the "boat people."

Often, the boat people had no idea where they would land or what would become of them. They

Many Vietnamese fled their homeland by boat at the end of the war.

hoped to be accepted as refugees in nearby countries, such as Malaysia, Indonesia, Thailand, or the Philippines. Along the way, they faced many dangers. Some boats were so heavily loaded with people that they sank. Other boats ran out of gasoline and drifted at the mercy of the sea. Many people starved to death or died from contagious diseases. Some experts estimate that almost half the people who started out from Vietnam died before they even reached land.

Vietnam Today

Today, Vietnam faces great difficulties. Floods and droughts have destroyed crops, and many people in the north have starved. The nation must struggle to repay heavy debts to the Soviet Union. The war with Cambodia also drained the country's funds. Vietnam's army is the fourth largest in the world, and the cost of supporting it takes more than half the nation's income.

The government is attempting reforms that it hopes will aid the economy. In the past, most people had to buy the things they needed from the illegal "black market." Today, new laws are encouraging a "free market" where individuals are allowed to sell fresh produce and other products.

Vietnam is trying to re-establish ties with Western nations. To improve relations, the government has withdrawn its troops from Cambodia. Although the U.S. government does not recognize the Socialist Republic of Vietnam, American tourists are now allowed to visit the country for the first time since 1975.

Even though Vietnam suffered great damage during its years of war, its people are still its greatest resource. They are proud of their ancient past and hope to turn Vietnam into a prosperous, thriving country.

5. Tales of Dragons and Swords

Throughout Vietnam are monuments built to honor the country's many heroes. Ho Chi Minh's tomb in Hanoi is one of the few new structures built in the city for thirty years. During the war, when a soldier died whose name was unknown, he was buried under a marker that read *liet si*, or "heroic soldier," instead of a name.

The Vietnamese enjoy telling stories about the adventures of their ancient heroes. Because in the past most Vietnamese peasants could not read or write, the stories of heroes were often passed on by word of mouth from older family members to young children. Filled with real people and real places, the stories have been changed over time and embroidered with touches of fantasy. Today, they still teach children some of Vietnam's ancient history, but mostly they are fun to hear!

Magic Animals

One of Vietnam's most famous heroes is Le Loi, founder of the fifteenth-century Le dynasty. According to legend, Le Loi was a simple fisherman who was sitting sadly beside a lake one day, thinking about how cruel Vietnam's Chinese rulers were. Suddenly, a giant turtle

Ho Chi Minh's tomb in Hanoi.

appeared in the lake, bearing a magic sword that gave Le Loi superhuman powers. With this sword, he led the Vietnamese people to victory, using guerrilla warfare and elephants to defeat the Chinese army. After he had established peace, Le Loi returned to the lake and threw the sword back to the magic turtle. Today, that lake is called *Ho Hoan Kiem*—Lake of the Returned Sword— and is the centerpiece of a beautiful park in Hanoi. In the middle of the lake rises an ancient monument honoring Le Loi. Some northern Vietnamese believe that the magic turtle still lives in Ho Hoan Kiem, and that it appeared briefly on the day Ho Chi Minh died.

Besides the giant turtle, other magic animals appear in Vietnamese myths. Dragons are the wisest and luckiest of them all. The chief dragon lives in the sky and controls clouds, fog, wind, and rain. When the dragon breathes, his breath forms clouds, which may turn into rain. He has horns on his head, eagle-claws on his five toes, and a beard. He is very fond of jewels and jade, and he carries a bright pearl under his chin.

The phoenix—a bird with a colorful, long tail—is the symbol of happiness and good fortune. In one legend, the phoenix and the dragon found a shiny white stone and worked together to shape it into a bright pearl. Over time, they grew to love each other. The dragon and phoenix are often pictured together, with the bright pearl between them. The phoenix is also a common decoration on the woman's garment called an *ao dai*.

Chewing the Betel

Many Vietnamese folktales try to explain the origin of everyday things or events. The ancient custom of "chewing the betel"—a gesture of friendship—is part of weddings and other ceremonies, and is common among some older women. They take a nut from an areca palm tree, wrap it in a betel vine leaf, sprinkle it with quicklime, and chew it. The taste is tangy, and the dark red juice is spit out like tobacco juice. It turns their teeth dark, but older women believe it also makes the teeth stronger. One story tells how chewing the betel began.

According to legend, there once lived two handsome brothers, Tan and Lang, who were identical in good looks and good manners, even though they were not the same age. When their parents died, the brothers moved in with a generous mandarin, or rich official. He admired their grace and goodness so much that he offered his daughter's hand in marriage to whoever claimed to be the older brother. But Tan and Lang loved each other dearly, and each insisted that the other brother take the beautiful maiden.

To find out who was the oldest, the mandarin served two delicious bowls of food, but only one pair of chopsticks. Quickly, with great respect, Lang handed the chopsticks to Tan, proving that Tan was the older brother.

Tan married the mandarin's lovely daughter and soon grew to love her so much that he neglected his brother. With a broken heart, Lang ran away until he came to the sea. There, he sat down and cried until he died and was changed into a chalky white rock. When Tan discovered his brother had run away, he felt great sorrow and shame. He went to the same spot on the shore, sat down, and cried until he was turned into an areca palm tree. Soon the beautiful, sad wife followed her husband's trail to the same place. She wept until she, too, died and was turned into a betel vine, which climbed lovingly around the palm tree.

Years later, everything died in a drought except the betel vine and the palm tree. Seeing this, the emperor declared that the mixture of betel vine, areca nut, and limestone would be a symbol of brotherly and wifely love. Brothers and sisters began to chew the mixture as a sign of caring, and newlyweds began to use it in their wedding ceremonies.

A Vietnamese Cinderella

In some Vietnamese folktales, people learn a lesson. One of the most popular is the Vietnamese version of Cinderella. In the Vietnamese version, a girl named Tam lived with her selfish stepmother and stepsister named Cam. Tam was beautiful and kind, but her ugly stepmother and stepsister made her do all the chores.

One day, a kind fairy gave Tam a magic fish, which she raised in a well and took care of lovingly. Jealous, the greedy stepmother and Cam caught the fish and ate him. While Tam was weeping over the loss of her little friend, the fairy appeared again and told Tam to bury

This painting shows a portion of the Vietnamese legend about Tam and Cam.

the fish bones, wait ten days, and then dig them up.

Tam waited anxiously. On the tenth day, instead of bones, she found lovely new clothes and the most beautiful pair of slippers she had ever seen. They were made of the finest cloth, woven with fantastic designs in golden thread and sparkling beads and jewels.

Tam kept the slippers carefully hidden, but one day she wore them while taking the water buffalo out to graze and got them wet. She put each slipper on a buffalo horn to dry. Suddenly, a raven swooped down out of the sky and snatched up one slipper. The raven carried the slipper far away and dropped it in the court-yard of a young, handsome prince. The prince had never seen such a marvelous work of art. He decided that whoever owned the slipper would be worthy to be his bride. His father, the emperor, announced that he would hold a festival to find the owner of the slipper.

The stepmother and Cam excitedly planned what fancy clothes they would wear to the festival. The cruel stepmother told Tam she had to stay home and separate out the black beans that were mixed up with white beans in an enormous basket. Tam's heart sank when she saw the task, yet she quietly began to work. Seeing this, the kind fairy sent a flock of friendly blackbirds to separate the beans for her. Within moments, the task was done. Tam put on her lovely new clothes and—carrying the other jeweled slipper—rushed off to the festival.

All the women in the kingdom were waiting to try on the slipper, but their feet were all too big, especially Cam's. Tam tried on the shoe, which fit perfectly. Then she brought out the matching slipper and put it on, too! The prince fell in love with her, and they were married.

Out of jealousy, the stepmother and Cam killed Tam, and told the prince it was an accident. Through magic, Tam was turned into a nightingale, a tree, and a fruit, before she was finally reunited with the prince.

The cruel stepmother and stepsister were driven from the kingdom forever, but Tam and the prince lived together in happiness for the rest of their lives.

Vietnamese stories might be about a beautiful fairy princess on an enchanted mountain, or about a brave hero who really lived, yet the children of Vietnam enjoy hearing them all. Gathered around a lantern at home, they listen as the grandmother weaves a magical tale. It is one way that the Vietnamese bring their families closer together and pass on ancient traditions.

6. *Fireworks for Fun*

The people of Vietnam enjoy celebrating special occasions. Some of these celebrations are religious, others honor famous heroes, and still others celebrate changes in the seasons. A few celebrations are so popular that the entire country observes them, while many others are held only in certain towns or regions. Officially, the government recognizes only five public holidays—days in which government employees do not have to work. These holidays are New Year's Day on January 1, the lunar new year festival called *Tet*, and three patriotic holidays: Liberation Day, May Day, and National Day.

Tet

Traditionally, the Vietnamese have followed the Chinese lunar calendar, which begins each new month at the time of the new moon. On this calendar, the beginning of the new year falls sometime between late January and early February. The date varies because months on a lunar calendar are shorter than the months in a Western calendar.

Today, Vietnam uses the same twelve-month calendar as Western nations. January 1 is officially called

New Year's Day. Although some people celebrate this one-day government holiday, Tet is still observed as the traditional new year's. It is by far the most important holiday of the year. During Tet, government employees get three days off, and schools close.

The Tet festival started thousands of years ago. Ancient Vietnamese farmers held joyful feasts and ceremonies to thank the gods that spring had arrived again and to pray that the new crops would be successful. Today during Tet, the Vietnamese visit friends and relatives, watch colorful parades and dances, and prepare for a new year. Dressed in their best clothes, they eat fancy meals, play games, give gifts, and forget about their worries for awhile.

Preparations for Tet begin weeks beforehand. In Vietnam, a tree called *hoa mai* blooms with lovely, delicate yellow blossoms in the early spring. About two weeks before Tet—while the limbs of the tree are still bare—people snip a cutting off the tree, singe its bottom with fire, and place it in a jar of water in the house. If the family is lucky, the hoa mai will bloom in time for Tet, bringing good fortune to the house. In some regions of the country, the Vietnamese also place cheerful branches of pink peach blossoms on their doors. These blossoms are a symbol of the rebirth of spring and the promise of a new beginning.

Just before Tet, people often hire scholars, called

thay do, to write new year's greetings in the ancient method of writing the Vietnamese language, called *chu nom*. People hang these long, red strips of paper on their front doors.

During Tet, many people return to the village of their birth. There, they spend time with relatives and old friends, and visit the tombs of their ancestors. Families sweep the grave sites clean and prepare them for the spirits of ancestors, because they believe the spirits will return to earth during Tet. At home, people decorate the family altars with flowers, fresh fruit, food, and incense for the visiting spirits. They pray that the spirits will travel safely to and from the house, by way of the newly cleaned tombs.

Some Vietnamese families also prepare their homes for the visit of Ong Tao, a kitchen god who is guardian of the hearth. A Vietnamese legend says that Ong Tao visits kitchens during Tet to inspect the family's housekeeping. If everything is in order, Ong Tao will give a favorable report to the Jade Emperor, the ruler of all the gods, and the family will have good luck all year. To make certain the report will be good, women put their kitchens in order and leave out special gifts of fruit, honey, paper clothing, and a paper carp, or fish, for Ong Tao to ride back to the home of the gods.

Dragons are also thought to roam the earth during Tet. Spotting one is another way to have good luck all

A Vietnamese scholar paints good luck banners in the ancient chu nom *language.*

year. In public Tet celebrations, a colorful dragon made of papier-mâché and cloth is paraded through the community by young men, who hide under the cloth body. The dragon bobs and weaves as it dances down the street, visiting shops to bring them good luck. Shop owners hang gifts of vegetables or money from their roofs for the dragon to take. Afterward, thousands of firecrackers explode like thunder to ward off evil spirits.

People may follow many traditional beliefs to try to increase their luck during Tet. When sweeping up the red bits of firecracker debris from shops and homes, many people sweep inward rather than out the door, believing they will collect good fortune all year. Others will not sweep at all during Tet, for fear of sweeping prosperity out the door. Before Tet arrives, all debts must be cleared up. The Vietnamese believe that if you owe money on the lunar new year's, you will owe money all year long. In fact, most people believe that whatever happens during Tet will be repeated during the coming year. Children try to obey their parents, and not argue or say unkind things. Parents try not to scold their children or punish them.

The children's good behavior is rewarded by gifts of money, called *li-xi* or *tien mung tuoi*. They can use this money when playing games with friends and relatives, especially gambling games. Adults usually play card or dice games, but a favorite children's game is *bau-ca-tom-cua* ("pear-fish-shrimp-crab"), or animal chess.

To play this game, a large paper divided into six squares is laid out on the floor. Each square has a different picture on it—a fish, crab, shrimp, deer, rooster, or pear. There are three dice, and each side of the dice has one of these pictures on it. Children place their money on the square they want to bet on. The dealer shakes the three dice in a bowl, and then turns the bowl over on the floor. If the animal a player bets on shows on one of the dice, the dealer must pay the player the same amount bet on the square. If the animal shows on two or three dice, the dealer must pay double or triple what the player bet. Children—and sometimes adults—play this game for hours. It can become quite fast and lively!

Friends and families visit each other during Tet, traveling in a circle from house to house for good luck. Many people believe that the family's first visitor on new year's day will determine their luck for the rest of the year. For example, a man or woman whose father had recently died would bring bad luck.

Visitors express good wishes, give gifts, and feast on special foods, such as fried watermelon seeds, sweetened dried fruit, candy, pickled vegetables, *banh giay* (a specially prepared sticky rice), and *banh chung* (a square pastry wrapped in banana leaves, with a rich bean paste and pork inside). Small, round watermelons are popular, too. Many people believe that if the first watermelon cut open on Tet is bright red, the family will have good luck that year.

Patriotic Holidays

Besides January 1 and Tet, the Vietnamese government recognizes three national public holidays. May Day on May 1 is set aside to honor workers, similar to Labor Day in the United States. Towns and cities in Vietnam sponsor parades, speeches, and organized demonstrations. Individuals who have distinguished themselves by working hard may receive small awards or honorary titles such as "labor hero."

National Day in September is celebrated in memory of the day in 1945 when Ho Chi Minh read the Vietnamese Declaration of Independence. On this day, people give patriotic speeches and march in parades, particularly in Hanoi.

The third official holiday, April 30, is called Liberation of Saigon, or Liberation Day. It marks the day in 1975 when North Vietnam's Communist army marched into South Vietnam's capital of Saigon, and the country came under one rule. On this day, government employees hang the red Communist flag from windows and drape banners with slogans from buildings in Ho

Chi Minh City. April 30 is an important day for members of the Communist government. They use the word *liberate* rather than *capture* because they believe they were freeing the southerners from foreign rule. Many South Vietnamese do not agree with this, but they are not free to express their opinions.

Mid-Autumn Festival

Although the government recognizes only these five official holidays, the Vietnamese people celebrate many unofficial festivals as well. The favorite of many children is *Tet Trung-thu*, or Mid-Autumn Festival. It occurs in September, about the time of the fall harvest. Because the full moon appears at its largest and brightest during this celebration, some people also call it the Moon Festival.

During the days before Tet Trung-thu, many children make colorful lanterns out of thin rice paper and bamboo. Other children prefer to buy their lanterns already made. Some lanterns are round, some are long, some are shaped like fish or stars, and some have little figures of animals or people dancing inside. A candle is carefully placed in each lantern so that it glows brightly as it dangles from strings or from bamboo poles.

After dark, when the moon is large and yellow, the children gather to form a lantern parade. As the parade

Colorful lanterns are sold throughout Vietnam before the Mid-Autumn Festival.

moves slowly down the street, the children sing favorite songs. Parents and older brothers and sisters watch from the sidelines as the children pass by. Each child must hold his or her lantern very carefully, or the thin rice paper will catch on fire. By the end of the procession, many lanterns will be burnt up. It is quite an accomplishment for a child's lantern to last all the way until the end of the parade, especially on a windy night!

After the parade, the children go home, where their mothers and grandmothers have prepared plates of special sweetened rice cakes—called "moon cakes"—fried melon seeds, and other treats. Then, adults and children all go outside to admire the shining full moon with friends and relatives. On this evening, children may gather around their grandparents to hear favorite legends and fairy tales, such as one about Chu Cuoi, the "man in the moon." Because the Trung-thu festival is so much fun for children, some Vietnamese also call it the Children's Festival.

Festivals Honoring Heroes

Many Vietnamese festivals are held to honor the country's national heroes. During the Trung Sisters celebration, people remember the two famous sisters who overthrew the Chinese in A.D. 39 and then drowned themselves when they were defeated. This festival is held in villages and towns in several regions of the country. In each town, two girls are chosen to dress up in colorful costumes like those worn in the Trung Sisters' era. The girls ride an elephant down the street, accompanied by more costumed girls walking beside them. Even the elephant is decorated with colorful trim and an ornamented saddle! At this time, all Vietnamese can take pride in the contributions of women to Vietnam's history.

A similar festival is held only in the Vinh Phu province. Here, people honor Thieu Hoa, a female general in the army of the Trung sisters. In this celebration, a procession carries a statue of the village's guardian spirit to a pagoda, amid shouts, cheers, and the beating of gongs and loud drums. Behind the statue, people carry two colorfully decorated handmade elephants, representing the elephants ridden by the Trung sisters.

After the procession arrives at the pagoda, the villagers move to an open sports field to play *danh phet*. The game's leader carries a bright red ball to the field and puts it inside a deep hole. On a signal, young men and women rush to the hole and try to pick the ball out with bamboo sticks. The winner is the first person to stab the bamboo ball and carry it to a special marker. This game represents the way General Thieu Hoa trained her troops.

Although this festival takes place in only one province, towns and villages throughout the country honor their famous local heroes with similar celebrations. The Vietnamese enjoy celebrating many events. It is an opportunity for them to spend time with family and friends, and remember their country's ancient past.

7. *Honoring Family Ties*

In Vietnam, the family is the most important part of society. According to an ancient saying, "If you want to destroy our nation, you must first destroy the family." The recent war caused a lot of damage to Vietnamese family life. Some families that had lived in the same village for many generations were suddenly forced to move. Many families were torn apart when some members died and others went to foreign countries to live. Yet, in spite of all these hardships, families in Vietnam were not destroyed. They remain large, close-knit, and loyal.

Husband and Wife

Today, people in Vietnamese families relate in ways that have not changed much in thousands of years. The husband and father is head of the household, and he has the final authority in all family matters. Traditionally, he earns the family's income, while his wife manages it, buying food, clothes, and basic necessities for the entire family. She gives her husband only enough money for a few small personal items. In rural areas, both the wife and husband may work in the rice fields at times, but the man does the heavy plowing. The woman usually tends the vegetable garden, takes care of the children, cooks, and cleans.

The Vietnamese husband expects his wife and children to serve and respect him. He, in turn, is responsible for seeing that his children get the best education the family can afford. He will continue to help his sons with advice and money, even after they are grown, married, and living with their wives in his household. The father can punish his children in any way he sees fit, and they must ask his permission for many things.

Second in authority in the family is the oldest son. If the father dies, he takes over the father's duties. Younger brothers and sisters must often ask his permission before they can play or visit friends.

Girls are expected to serve and obey their fathers when they are young, their husbands when they are married, and their oldest son when they are widowed. In the past, women received less education than men because they were expected to take care of the house and the children. During the long years of war, though, many women were left without husbands or sons to help them, and they learned to manage their own businesses and finances. Today, the government has laws granting equality for women. More Vietnamese girls are now attending school and working in factories or as teachers and doctors.

Hard Work and Birthdays

Everyone in a Vietnamese family must work hard to help the family survive. Children have many chores to do, beginning at a very young age. Girls may help in the kitchen, clean house, wash clothes, and tend the vegetable garden. Boys fetch water, take care of the livestock, and help with the farming or fishing. Baby-sitters are not needed because older children watch the younger ones.

As they grow older, children in Vietnam do not celebrate their birthdays on the day they were born. Instead, everyone in the country is considered to be one year older at the lunar new year's festival of Tet, and people celebrate then. Only small babies are honored with special birthday celebrations—once when they are one month old, and again at one year old.

When a baby is one month old, the parents give a party to introduce it to family and friends, who bring gifts of clothes. In a traditional ceremony, twelve bowls of tapioca pudding and twelve bowls of steamed sweet rice are placed in two rows on a table. The grandfather blesses the child, wishes it luck in life, and everyone celebrates.

A child's first birthday is one of the most important events in his or her life. Relatives and friends arrive, bringing gifts of clothes, toys, jewelry, and money.

Again, twelve bowls of pudding and steamed rice are placed on the table. This time, the grandfather formally introduces the child to the gathering, using its given name.

Some Vietnamese families also try to tell the child's future. In front of the child they place a tray containing a comb, a flower, a pair of scissors, a pen or pencil, a ruler, and some steamed rice. According to the custom, the item the child grabs first will determine his or her fate. The scissors means the child will become a tailor; the comb—a barber; the ruler—an architect; the pen— a writer; the flower—a lover of pleasure. Grabbing the rice first means a life of hard work!

A Vietnamese child does not have to keep the name he or she was born with—many children change their given names around the age of twelve. The Vietnamese write their family name first, then their middle name, and finally their given name, the opposite of the way people write their names in the United States. For example, if a man signs his name Nguyen Van Anh, that means his last name is Nguyen, his middle name is Van, and his first name is Anh. There are only a few family names in Vietnam because in the past people often changed their name to that of the emperor as a sign of respect. About one-third of all Vietnamese are named Nguyen because the Nguyen family ruled during the last empire.

Wedding Excitement

To the Vietnamese, a wedding is an important family occasion. Today, young people may choose their own husbands or wives, although the young man must still ask permission from the young woman's father to marry her. A special matchmaking couple then makes all the wedding arrangements. The matchmakers are usually an older couple who have been married many years and are respected in the community.

The two families are introduced in an engagement party at the future bride's house. The matchmaking couple consults astrologers—people who believe they can tell the future based on the position of the stars—to choose the most favorable day for this party. In a special ceremony, the wife of the matchmaker presents the bride's mother and future mother-in-law with an areca nut wrapped in a betel leaf and quicklime. The matchmaker then presents rice wine to the girl's father and future father-in-law. The groom brings his future wife a tray full of engagement jewelry, mostly gold. Friends and relatives also bring gifts, but only in even numbers—one of anything would bring bad luck.

If all goes well, the couple decides on a favorable wedding date, again by consulting astrologers. The bride wears a red or pink ao dai, and the groom wears a blue one. The groom, his family, and friends meet at the

These young women are members of a Vietnamese wedding party.

bride's house, where the women again accept betel leaves and the men drink rice wine. The matchmaker lights two red candles before the family's altar, and the bride and groom bow and exchange rings. The matchmaker then binds their hands with a pink thread as a symbol of happiness. The couple eats a piece of ginseng dipped in salt as a symbol of difficulties in their future life. After bowing again, the matchmakers announce that the couple is married. The newly married couple, family, and friends then travel to the groom's house for a feast and reception.

Not all couples follow the elaborate steps of a traditional wedding, especially in the larger cities. City brides often wear Western-style wedding gowns, and Catholic couples may have a church ceremony. In cities, couples may also travel from the bride's home to the reception in a rented car decorated with colorful garlands of flowers.

Honoring Ancestors

Another important time when Vietnamese families get together is to honor the anniversary of an ancestor's death. When someone dies in Vietnam, relatives wear loose, white clothing and a white headband at the funeral. Families who can afford it rent elaborately decorated wagons to carry the relatives to the grave sites.

Most people, though, can only afford a small procession, with a few people beating drums and hitting gongs as they parade through the street.

One hundred days after the death, a large feast is held. Relatives travel from all over to attend. The favorite foods of the honored ancestor are placed in front of the altar. Family members bow to express their respect, and then everyone enjoys a big feast. Every year after this, a celebration is held on the anniversary of the ancestor's death.

The Vietnamese Kitchen

Food is important in all Vietnamese celebrations, and Vietnam's cooking is known around the world. The Vietnamese eat rice every day, usually with vegetables. Meat is often not available, but when it is, fish, seafood, pork, and duck are favorites.

The Vietnamese serve rice in many ways—plain, sweetened with coconut, floating in soups, fried with vegetables and meat, or ground into flour and made into buns, noodles, or rice paper. Each kind of noodle has its own name. *Mien* are tiny, clear noodles; *bun* are white-colored noodles; and *pho* are brittle noodles, also called "rice sticks." Noodles can be fried, used in egg rolls, or mixed with meat and vegetables. Sometimes they are even served for breakfast in a soup also called *pho.* This soup is so popular it can be called the national food of Vietnam.

Rice paper is so thin you can almost see through it and so brittle it would fall to pieces if you dropped it. Yet after rice paper has been dipped in water, it becomes very soft, like a piece of sheer cloth. Meat and vegetables can be rolled up inside it. The famous *cha gio*, or Vietnamese egg rolls, are made this way and then deep-fried until they are crispy.

Vietnamese food can be very spicy and hot, with hot peppers, garlic, star anise, ginger, and lemongrass. The most important ingredient in Vietnamese cooking is *nuoc mam*, or fish sauce. It is made from layers of fish and salt which have been placed in large vats and fermented for nine to twelve months.

In Vietnam, meats and vegetables are usually cut up and served in small portions because the Vietnamese use *dua*, or chopsticks, instead of a knife and fork. Most cooking is done on small, three-legged stoves that use wood or coal for heat. Cooks usually shop for their foods at open-air markets, where baskets of fruit and vegetables line the street.

Many Vietnamese meals are time-consuming to prepare, but you can make a simple Vietnamese meal with only a little help from an adult. For the main dish, *goi cuon*—a type of meat and vegetable roll—is easy to prepare. Asian food stores in most American cities

An open-air market in Hanoi.

carry the ingredients needed for this delicious meal.

Goi Cuon

1 cup shrimp (frozen shrimp is the easiest to use)
1 cup pork, sliced
water
a handful of rice stick noodles
1/2 cup mint leaves (not the fuzzy spearmint leaves)
1 bunch coriander or cilantro
1 head leaf lettuce
round rice paper (small size)

Follow these steps to make the stuffing for the goi cuon:

1. Place the shrimp and pork each in a separate saucepan. Cover each with water, and boil until the shrimp and pork are tender. Drain the water, and set each aside while you prepare the other ingredients.
2. Boil about one cup of water in a medium saucepan. Add the handful of rice stick noodles. Remove the pan from the heat, and let it sit for a few minutes until the noodles are soft and white. Drain off the extra water. Set the noodles aside.

3. On a cutting board, slice the boiled shrimp and boiled pork into very thin strips. Chop the mint leaves, coriander, and lettuce into little pieces. Set these ingredients aside.

Follow these steps to form the goi cuon rolls:

4. Quickly dip a sheet of rice paper into a bowl of water. Shake the water off, and lay the rice paper aside for several seconds until it is soft enough to roll.

5. In the center of the rice paper, put some shrimp, pork, and stick noodles. Sprinkle the mint, coriander, and lettuce over the top. (Don't put too much stuffing on the rice paper, or it will spill out as you roll.)

6. Pick up the end of the rice paper nearest to you. Roll this end of the paper over the ingredients. Then, fold the right and left ends of the paper over the ingredients in the middle. Finally, roll the goi cuon the rest of the way over—away from you—to form a tight roll.

7. Repeat steps 4-6 with a new piece of rice paper each time, until you run out of stuffing ingredients.

8. Place the goi cuon rolls on a platter and serve. They should be eaten while they are fresh. Goi cuon rolls do not keep overnight.

In Vietnam, goi cuon rolls are served with a special sauce called *nuoc cham.* This sauce is made from the nuoc mam fish sauce and is served in a separate bowl on the table. Diners spoon the sauce over their rolls or dip the rolls into the sauce before eating. Nuoc cham is also served with many other Vietnamese dishes.

Nuoc Cham Sauce

3 tablespoons nuoc mam fish sauce (can be bought at Asian food stores)
1 cup water
1/3 cup white vinegar
1/3 cup sugar
1 teaspoon very finely chopped garlic (about 2 cloves)
1/2 cup shredded carrots

Combine the fish sauce, water, vinegar, sugar, and garlic in a bowl. Stir until the sugar is dissolved. Add the carrots. Nuoc cham can be kept in the refrigerator in a tightly covered container for up to two weeks.

The Vietnam usually eat rice and a vegetable dish with their meals. You may wish to serve plain white rice with your goi cuon rolls. (Prepare the rice according to the directions on the package.) You may also serve one or both of the following dishes.

Fried Rice with Egg

2 tablespoons vegetable oil
2 cloves garlic, finely chopped
3 cups cold, cooked rice (prepared according to the package directions)
1 egg

1. Heat the oil in a skillet. Add the garlic, and cook it for about 1 minute, stirring constantly. Add the rice, and cook it for about 5-7 minutes over a medium heat, stirring constantly.
2. With a spoon, form a hole in the center of the rice. Break open the egg and drop it into this hole (without the shell). Mix the egg in with the rice until all the rice is coated with egg. It will look yellow. Stir for a few minutes, and remove the pan from the heat.
3. Spoon the rice into a large bowl and serve it with a separate bowl of nuoc cham sauce. This recipe serves four. Each diner can spoon nuoc cham sauce over his or her own portion of rice.

Stir-fried Cauliflower

1 head cauliflower, medium-sized
1 small onion
1 tablespoon vegetable oil
1/2 teaspoon pepper

1 tablespoon nuoc mam fish sauce (can be bought at Asian food stores)
1/4 cup chopped scallions (a type of small, green onions)

1. Break the cauliflower into bite-sized pieces. Slice the onion into round rings. Place all the ingredients beside the stove. (This recipe cooks very quickly, and you won't have time to stop and find anything.)
2. In a large skillet, heat the oil over a high heat. Add the onion. Fry it over the high heat, stirring constantly, until the onion is tender.
3. Add the cauliflower. Cook it for 2-3 minutes, stirring constantly.
4. Add the pepper and fish sauce. Mix well. Cover the pan, and cook it for a couple of minutes, until the cauliflower is tender but still crisp. Add the scallions and stir.
5. Spoon the mixture into a large bowl and serve it hot. This recipe makes four portions. The Vietnamese often eat stir-fried vegetables with plain white rice.

The Vietnamese traditionally eat fresh fruit for dessert. At the end of your meal, you can arrange some fresh fruit on a platter and set it on the table. Then, everyone can enjoy a sweet ending to a delicious meal!

8. School, Service, and Sports

Throughout their history, the Vietnamese have respected and honored their scholars and teachers. Today, attending school is an important part of a child's life. Teachers and parents expect the students to study hard, receive good grades, and take their education seriously. Schools have no playground equipment, there are few activities outside the classroom, and only the high schools have sports teams. School life is very strict, and is centered on learning and studying.

Before 1975, Vietnam had both public and private schools—including those owned by the Catholic church—which charged a tuition. Today, the government owns all the schools, and education is free for everyone. The Department of Education is facing many problems, though, because the nation is very poor. There are not enough teachers, textbooks, and school buildings for the millions of students. Most school buildings used today were built by the French many years ago. They are often run-down and lack facilities.

Vietnam has one of the highest birth rates in the world, which means that more children reach school age every year. Yet the government cannot afford to build new schools, and young Vietnamese children must

A group of young boys prepares for martial arts class.

attend school in shifts. Some children attend school in the morning, from 7:00 A.M. to noon. Others attend in the afternoon, from 1:00 P.M. to 5:00 P.M. All students must go to school six days a week, from Monday through Saturday.

In some ways, schools in Vietnam are similar to those in the United States. The educational system includes elementary, middle, and high schools. Vietnam's school year starts in September and runs for nine months, with three months off for summer vacation.

In other ways, though, Vietnam's situation is much different. According to law, children must begin school at age five. Yet many do not begin until six or seven because their parents are too poor to afford the few school supplies, such as notebooks, that are needed. Especially in rural areas, children must often work rather than attend school, to earn money to help supply the family's basic needs. In spite of these problems, most Vietnamese complete elementary school. Although many later leave school to work, four out of every five Vietnamese can read and write.

Elementary School

Most Vietnamese children walk to school because there are no buses. Sometimes an adult may give a child a ride to school on a bicycle, but children rarely own their own bicycles. In Vietnam, bicycles are used for transportation, not fun.

Once the students arrive at school, each class forms a line outside the building, as straight and perfect as possible. The teachers carefully inspect each line. The one which is straightest and quietest gets to march inside first. After school, the lines will form again, and this time the straightest line is allowed to go home first.

When the homeroom teacher arrives, the students

stand up and greet him or her. They sing a patriotic song and then recite a pledge to study hard and honor their teachers and parents. If a student cannot recite the pledge, he or she may be expelled from school.

The Vietnamese study some of the same subjects as students in the United States, such as mathematics, science, history, social studies, and languages. Before 1975, many Vietnamese children studied French. Today, they have a choice between Russian and English as their second language. Children remain in the same classroom all day, but their teachers change with each subject. Some subjects are taught every day, while others are taught only once or twice a week.

Vietnamese teachers are very strict. Each class usually begins with an oral examination—the teacher calls upon a student, who must stand and answer the question. If the student misses the question, he or she may have to write the correct answer fifty or more times. Sometimes, the teacher sends the student to stand in a corner and think about the answer. The student must remain in the corner until he or she can answer correctly. In small rural villages, boys who misbehave must sometimes kneel on a large fruit called a *sau rieng*, or durian. The outer shell of this fruit is hard and nobby, creating a lot of pain in the knees.

About midway through the school shift, the children take a short break. During this time they may eat a snack, if they have brought one. In some cities, vendors sell fruit, vegetables, or sweets to schoolchildren. Many children are too poor to buy anything and do not get to eat. Other children bring snacks from home, usually fruit or rice pressed into "cakes." These cakes are often wrapped in banana leaves to keep them from drying out.

In some cities, the schools take a thirty-minute break, with the first fifteen minutes spent exercising in the schoolyard. Other schools have only a fifteen-minute break, and the children are not allowed outside. Instead, they go to a large, empty room where they can walk around and visit with friends.

At the beginning of the school year, each class of about sixty students is divided into clean-up groups, which take turns cleaning the school. When it is a group's turn for clean-up duty, the students arrive early to clean the blackboards, sweep the rooms, and empty the trash cans.

Every Monday, students listen to the principal give a thirty-minute speech before classes begin. At the end of the week—on Saturday—students stand in front of the teacher and tell what they have learned during the week. Students in Vietnamese schools do not receive grades such as *A, B,* or *C* for each subject. Instead, each child is ranked in his or her class—the student with the highest grades is ranked number one, and so on. About

once a month, the teacher sends a report to the parents telling them the rank of their children and explaining which subjects need more work. At the end of the school year, the three top-ranked students in each classroom get rewards, such as notebooks, pencils, erasers, calendars, rulers, or merit badges. Top students often join a society called *thieu nien tien phong*, or "young pioneers."

About once a year, children may take a field trip, usually to a museum, historical site, or monument. Students in larger towns sometimes go to a movie on their field trip. At the end of the year, each school has a farewell program. Selected students sing traditional songs, dance Vietnamese folk dances, and perform in plays.

School and Work

Not all Vietnamese children attend middle school and high school, especially in the countryside where they must work to help their families survive. Those who do finish middle school must pass very difficult examinations before going on to high school. Students in high school study very hard. They know that they will obtain better jobs with a high school education, and that only the best students may be allowed to attend college. Students who cannot attend middle

A Vietnamese schoolgirl in her Young Pioneer outfit.

school or high school may attend one of Vietnam's many vocational schools. Here, they learn manual skills and trades such as carpentry, agriculture, and mechanics.

A boy or girl in high school is expected to help the community. Some students join an organization called the Ho Chi Minh Communist Youth Union. One of the main branches of this union is the Young Volunteers Force, which performs civic duties and takes part in reconstruction projects. Some members build houses and other buildings, plant trees to restore war-damaged forests, or tend crops such as pepper, coffee, citrus, sugarcane, ginger, or rubber trees. Other members have built roads, raised livestock, created shrimp farms, processed fish, or produced turpentine. In the far north, students even work in coal mines.

Although this organization is called a volunteer force, students do not have a choice in where they go or what project they work on. One former high school student, Hung, recalls his experiences in a similar program in Binh Dinh, in southern Vietnam. About once every three months, his entire class was taken to a jungle about a hundred miles away from his village. Under the supervision of their teacher, they built wooden sleeping platforms. These had to be raised off the ground to protect the students from animals. The boys then cut down trees, pulled up vines and undergrowth, and burned them in order to clear the land for farming. The girls gathered food and firewood, cooked, and cleaned.

The students worked hard all day, starting at 5:00 A.M. After clearing the land, they plowed it and planted crops. At the end of the long, hard day they slept on the platform beds. At the end of two weeks, they returned home, and the next class took over their duties.

High school students who pass difficult examinations may attend college. According to the government, Vietnam has ninety-three universities and other institutions of higher education. The two largest universities—the University of Ho Chi Minh City and the University of Hanoi—were both established by the French. Some college students travel to other Communist countries to earn degrees in high-technology fields. Unfortunately, Vietnam lacks computer-related or other high-technology industries, and many foreign-educated graduates cannot find jobs in their fields.

Most young Vietnamese men serve in the military. Afterward, they receive a small monthly pension from the government. Because jobs are often difficult to find, this pension can be an important source of income.

Sports and Recreation

Physical education is not taught as a subject in

These children are inventing their own game using small pebbles.

most Vietnamese elementary and middle schools. For fun, younger children often play games such as kick ball, jump rope, and marbles, or they invent games using stones or seeds. Because most families are poor, children must often substitute homemade items for the proper equipment in their games. For example, they may use round stones instead of glass marbles, or a ball of wadded-up paper instead of a badminton birdie.

High schools, though, have sports teams, and the

most popular sport is *da banh*, or soccer. Students also enjoy playing volleyball, ping pong, and tennis, and running in track and field events. Each year, high school teams compete in a series of tournaments. Local winners go on to represent their town or city in district tournaments, and then in regional playoffs.

Vietnam's larger cities also sponsor sports teams, especially soccer. These teams not only play each other, but also teams from other Communist nations. Unlike the United States—where sports teams are privately owned and admission fees are charged—in Vietnam the government funds each city's team, and tournaments are free to the public.

Besides attending sports tournaments, Vietnamese families like to visit the many interesting sites of their country. They often cannot afford to travel far, though. In Hanoi, people frequently visit Ho Chi Minh's tomb. Along the northern coast, they enjoy sailing among the many small islands dotting Ha Long Bay. At Da Nang, people swim at the sparkling white beaches, such as China Beach, a popular recreation spot of American soldiers during the 1960s. Today, tourists from Communist nations vacation along these same beaches.

One of the most famous vacation areas in Vietnam is the mountainous region near the town of Da Lat. Wealthy French families once had lovely homes here because the weather in Da Lat is cooler during the

Vietnam has many beautiful beaches, providing cool relief from the humid weather.

summer than in most other locations in Vietnam.

Although Vietnamese families are often poor, their country is rich in natural beauty for the people to enjoy. Families often go on picnics or spend their free time with friends or relatives. Sharing time together is often more important than the activity. It is a quality that has helped the Vietnamese survive in good times and bad.

9. Good-bye, Vietnam—Hello, America

Since 1975, hundreds of thousands of Vietnamese refugees have come to the United States. The refugees came in two "waves"—the first immediately after the war ended, and the second several years later. On a smaller scale, this movement of people is still happening today, as Vietnamese continue to leave the country.

Fleeing Vietnam

It is difficult for most Americans to imagine the chaos of living in a country that is invaded by a conquering army. In 1975, as the North Vietnamese army attacked South Vietnam, more than a million people tried to escape. They abandoned their homes and businesses, loading their possessions on bicycles, trucks, wagons, or on their backs.

Hoang, a young Vietnamese woman, recalls it as one of the worst times of her life. She was eleven years old at the time, and living in Da Nang with her mother and brothers and sisters. As news of the approaching Communist army came over the radio, Hoang's family had to act fast. The mother sold her rice shops for a price much less than their worth. The family left, taking what they could carry, including all the money they owned.

At first, they tried to rent a cyclo, but the drivers charged extremely high prices. Hoang and her family decided to walk to the beach where they had heard that American naval ships were taking refugees to safety. They had to bribe several soldiers before they reached the main road leading to the sea. There were thousands of people already on the road, pushing to get ahead.

When Hoang's family reached the beach, it was covered with people desperate to get on board the large U.S. ship in the harbor. Some people tried to sail to the ship in anything that would float—fishing boats, large baskets, and even inner tubes. Many jumped into the ocean and tried to swim out, only to drown in the choppy waves. Hoang could see people falling off the side of the ship as they tried to climb up the rope ladders. That day, the ships rescued 28,000 people.

Hoang's family found a place on a small cargo barge that was already crowded with more than two hundred people. For several days and nights, the barge sailed south along the coast. The people on board had no food or water. A number of them died, especially small children and the elderly.

When they reached shore, they were still in Vietnam. Hoang's mother paid a lot of money for space on a boat that would take them even farther away. In the panic of loading, the family got separated. Hoang could not find her mother, but she could see one of her brothers on a boat pulling away. Hoang began crying, until suddenly she saw her mother, who had refused to get on the departing boat without her. The mother had to spend most of their money for another boat.

The boat took them around the southern tip of Vietnam to an island where they joined thousands of other refugees, including the rest of Hoang's family. The island was overcrowded, and many people were sick. Life there left the people with bad memories. Men who had guns took food that was supposed to be given to the refugees and often sold it back to them for high prices. They also raped and molested many women.

People cheered when an American ship arrived to rescue them. There was not enough room on the ship for all the refugees, and hundreds of them began climbing the rope ladders at once. Some mothers even tossed their babies up to relatives who had already boarded the ship. A child's chance of survival was not good if it remained on the island, but many of the babies fell into the ocean and died.

Hoang's family was lucky. They all got onto the ship and were taken to a refugee camp in Guam, an island in the Pacific Ocean. Before long, her family was on its way to the United States and a new life.

In many ways, the second wave of refugees had a harder time. They set out to sea in boats—some very

Vietnamese children in a refugee camp.

small—and often drifted for weeks without food or water before being rescued. Some nations refused to allow them to land or put them in camps similar to prisons. A large number of refugees are still living in camps today. But other nations allowed Vietnamese refugees to start a new life within their borders. The U.S. government and American organizations such as World Vision helped more refugees than any other nation.

To Begin Again

The majority of the Vietnamese refugees arrived in America with few possessions—sometimes only the clothes on their backs. When they first arrived, they were sent to reception centers located at military bases. There, they studied English, received job training, and began learning about American culture until a sponsor could be located.

At first, the United States government attempted to spread the refugees equally over the entire country. Some moved to large cities such as New York, and others to small towns where they were the only Vietnamese. Some refugees were even sent to cold northern states—even though they had never seen snow! But this policy did not work because it separated many Vietnamese families and made the refugees feel isolated.

As soon as possible, the Vietnamese began moving to communities where other Vietnamese were living. Many preferred to live in California, where thousands of Asians with cultures more familiar to them already lived. Vietnamese fishermen migrated to Texas and the Gulf Coast, where they could fish as they had in their homeland. By 1986, the majority of Vietnamese Americans lived in California, with Texas second in numbers, and Washington state third.

Although most refugees began their lives in the

United States with government assistance, the average Vietnamese family stopped receiving federal help within three years. Instead, these new immigrants found jobs and became self-supporting as soon as possible.

Learning the American Way

Most newly arrived Vietnamese refugees spoke little English and knew nothing about the American way of life. Some things that Americans take for granted and use everyday were strange and complicated to the Vietnamese. On the other hand, many of the things the refugees did seemed strange to the Americans.

Hoang, the eleven-year-old girl who escaped from Da Nang in 1975, was excited when her family arrived in Pennsylvania. She was eager to see this land called America that she had heard so much about.

At first, everything was mysterious. Electric can openers, supermarkets, and fast-food restaurants amazed her. The food was strange, and her family missed her mother's cooking because she could not find some of the ingredients she needed to make Vietnamese food.

School presented several problems for Hoang. Although she was now twelve, she was placed in a lower grade because she didn't speak English well. But Hoang studied hard and soon learned enough English to be

A Vietnamese shrimper off the Gulf Coast of Texas.

promoted to the same grade as other children her age.

Hoang's name caused another problem. In Vietnam, the family name is written first and the given name last. Hoang's full name was Pham Thi Hoang, but many teachers and classmates called her Pham until she could make them understand that her given name was Hoang. Still, some children made fun of her name. She finally changed it to Linda so she would fit in better.

Since women in Vietnam keep their maiden names after marrying, Hoang's last name was not the same as her mother's, which is Nguyen. Some people drew the wrong conclusion from this difference, thinking that Hoang's mother was not married.

Although the family that sponsored her was kind and helpful, Hoang soon learned that not all Americans welcomed the Vietnamese. Some misinformed Americans called her a Communist, even though her family had risked their lives to get away from the Communists. Other Americans whose relatives or friends were killed in the war, blamed all Vietnamese for their loss.

Hoang's mother had problems at first, too. In Vietnam, she had been a successful businesswomen. But in America, Hoang's mother could not find work because she could not speak English well. She finally found a job on an assembly line. Here, she did skilled work with her hands and did not need to speak much English. She learned quickly and soon won several awards of excellence for her work.

As soon as possible, Hoang's family moved into a small apartment. Everyone old enough got a job and began saving money. Only six years after arriving in America with no possessions, the family members were able to combine their money and buy a nice house.

Going Into Business

The story of Hoang and her family is typical of many Vietnamese who came to America. They worked hard to earn their homes and jobs, but it was not easy. At first, many Vietnamese took jobs that other Americans did not want, such as late-night shifts at all-night convenience stores. Some Americans complained that the Vietnamese were taking away their jobs, but the store owners often defended the Vietnamese because they were such hard workers. Today, some of the same Vietnamese who used to work in convenience stores have saved their money and bought their own stores.

Along the Gulf Coast, many Vietnamese fishermen and shrimpers ran into problems with American fishermen who felt that they were not competing fairly. This conflict became violent at times. As time passed, though, the Vietnamese learned the ways of the American fishermen, and the tension lessened.

But only a minority of the Vietnamese had problems as severe as the Gulf Coast immigrants. Most refugees found jobs and worked hard to save money. The dreams of Vietnamese Americans were not much different than the dreams of other Americans—to own their own homes and businesses and have a secure future for their children. Many Vietnamese reached their goals, but not overnight. For years, Vietnamese families might save money by living in cheap apartments, and having few possessions. They worked long hours, often holding two or more jobs. Family members combined their incomes to buy food or clothing.

Over time, these families could afford to buy homes in middle-class neighborhoods, or businesses such as restaurants, grocery stores, beauty shops, or jewelry stores. In cities with a large Vietnamese population, entire Vietnamese malls or shopping centers appeared. Although most customers are Vietnamese, some restaurants are popular among Amerians who have developed a taste for Vietnamese food.

Helping Each Other

Vietnamese Americans feel that it is important to maintain contact with other Vietnamese. Places with large Vietnamese populations often have Vietnamese newspapers, magazines, radio stations, and television

A Vietnamese shopping mall near Houston offers a variety of Vietnamese goods.

programs. These news sources help keep the Vietnamese informed about their native land and about Vietnamese all over the world.

Another way Vietnamese keep informed is through organized groups such as the Vietnamese American Association, the Vietnamese Buddhist Association, the Vietnamese Doctor Association, and the Vietnamese Student Association. Many local groups have also been formed to help new refugees coming to America. These groups provide services such as English classes, job counseling, housing assistance, and legal services.

The Vietnamese Association helps reunite family members by keeping a record of refugees' addresses. It also promotes Vietnamese cultural events such as public Tet festivals. In Houston, a Vietnamese senior citizens organization helps preserve its culture by having older Vietnamese teach children traditional cooking, folk dancing, and musical instruments.

Vietnamese families in America have not forgotten their relatives who stayed behind in Vietnam. Many Vietnamese-American families send money and supplies to family members still in their native land. Some people in Vietnam today might not survive without the help of their friends and relatives in the United States.

The Changing Family

Today, there are many problems facing the Vietnamese-American community that have no easy solutions. The most serious of these stem from the differences in the values of traditional Vietnamese families compared to those of American culture. In their native land, Vietnamese family members lived together, with all working for the benefit of the whole family. Older people were respected, women obeyed their husbands and stayed home with the children, and divorce was

Vietnamese Americans in Texas celebrate Tet.

rare. In the United States, family members usually want
to be independent. Many teenagers move out of the
house as soon as they are eighteen, mothers frequently
work outside the home, and grandparents often live far
away from the rest of the family. Although Vietnamese
parents in the United States may wish to raise their
children with traditional values, the children—who
were often born and raised here—may be more influenced by the society they see around them.

The traditional Vietnamese father is head of the family. He makes all its decisions and often teaches the children. Because Vietnamese-American children often speak better English than their parents, many fathers are forced to rely on their children to read documents and help them with adult affairs. Some fathers think that they have lost respect in the eyes of their children. The young people may think they are smarter than their parents because they understand American ways better.

Vietnamese parents expect their children to be obedient and respectful, doing chores and studying hard. This is often difficult for Vietnamese children when they see their American classmates have what appears to be much more freedom. Vietnamese-American children may try hard to be accepted by their classmates and become American in their life-style. They may be more interested in rock music and movies than listening to their parents talk about a country they never saw or cannot remember.

Still, many Vietnamese-American young people are serious about their schoolwork because they see it as a way to become successful. Many graduate at the top of their class and score high on nationwide tests. Vietnamese names are often among the top winners at science and math fairs. Many have graduated with honors from well-known American universities.

Larger cities have another problem—Vietnamese youth gangs. Gang members may come from families where the traditional values fell apart. Members of some Vietnamese communities are trying to deal with this problem by getting the gang members to return to school, or helping them find jobs.

Many Vietnamese refugees came to the United States with a burning desire to be free. Most left their country with great sadness because they were leaving behind families, friends, and a culture that had existed for four thousand years. They may have felt as if they left part of themselves in the mountains and hills, the fishing villages and crowded cities, and the waving fields of green rice.

But they also brought a part of Vietnam with them to pass on to their children. In time, some Vietnamese traditions may blend into American culture, as traditions brought from other nations have. Today, the Vietnamese contribute to American society by being hard workers, excellent students, and shrewd businesspeople. Their children are part of America's hope for a better future.

Glossary

ao dai—a long, tight-fitting garment which is split up the sides and worn over pants

banh chung—a rice pastry wrapped in banana leaves, with a rich bean and pork paste inside

banh giay—a sweet, sticky rice dessert

bau-ca-tom-cua—a children's gambling game, also called "animal chess"

bun—a type of white-colored noodle

cai liem—a knife with a curved blade, used to cut rice stalks

cha gio—Vietnamese egg rolls

chan trau—a person who takes care of a water buffalo

chu nom—an ancient method of writing Vietnamese using Chinese characters

con trau—a water buffalo

cyclo—a three-wheeled bicycle with a passenger seat in front, used as a taxi

da banh—soccer

Dai Viet—the name given to Vietnam during its nine hundred years of independence, beginning in A.D. 969

danh phet—a game played during a festival in the Vinh Phu province

dong—the Vietnamese unit of money

don ganh—a device used to carry heavy loads; it consists of a long bamboo pole with a basket hanging from each end, balanced over the shoulder

dua—chopsticks

goi cuon—a type of meat and vegetable roll

hoa mai—a tree whose yellow blossoms are displayed during the festival of *Tet*

liet si—a heroic soldier

li-xi—gifts of money given to children during the festival of *Tet*

ma—a rice seedling

mien—a type of tiny, clear noodle

moi—the name once given to the mountain tribes in Vietnam; it means "savages"

nam—south

nam tien—"marching south"; the policy followed in the ancient Vietnamese empires of expanding the country's borders by conquering lands to the south

Nam Viet—the name given to the first Vietnamese empire, in 208 B.C.

Ngan-Ha—in Vietnamese mythology, the Silver River in the sky where the Jade Emperor, the ruler of the gods, lived; Americans call it the Milky Way

non la—a cone-shaped hat woven from leaves

nuoc cham—a sauce served with most Vietnamese meals; it is made with *nuoc mam*

nuoc mam—a fermented fish sauce; one of the main ingredients in Vietnamese cooking

pho—a type of brittle noodle; also the name of a popular soup

quoc ngu—a method of writing Vietnamese using letters of the Roman alphabet and accent marks to indicate tones

sau rieng—a type of fruit, also called a "durian"

tai chi chuan—a slow-moving form of martial art which emphasizes deep breathing and relaxing

Tet—a festival celebrating the lunar new year and the arrival of spring

Tet Trung-thu—the Mid-Autumn Festival, celebrated in September when the moon is at its brightest; also called the Children's Festival or Moon Festival

thay do—a highly educated scholar who is often consulted for advice and who is also able to write *chu nom*, the ancient method of writing Vietnamese

thieu nien tien phong—"young pioneers"; the name of a national organization for young people

tien mung tuoi—gifts of money given to children during the festival of *Tet*

Viet—an ancient race of people who are the ancestors of the modern Vietnamese

Viet Cong—a Communist guerrilla group active in South Vietnam during the Vietnam War

Vietminh—an organization of Vietnamese nationalists who fought the French during the French Indochinese War

Selected Bibliography

Doyle, Edward, Samuel Liscomb, and Stephen Weiss. *The Vietnam Experience.* 15 volumes. Boston: Boston Publishing, 1984.

Graetz, Rick. *Vietnam: Opening Doors to the World.* Helena, Montana: American Geographic Publishing, 1988.

Haskins, James. *Vietnamese Boat People.* Hillside, New Jersey: Enslow Publishers, 1980.

Hauptly, Denis J. *In Vietnam.* New York: Atheneum, 1985.

Karnow, Stanley. *Vietnam: A History.* New York: Viking Press, 1983.

Lawson, Don. *An Album of the Vietnam War.* New York: Franklin Watts, 1986.

_____. *The War in Vietnam.* New York: Franklin Watts, 1981.

Newman, Bernard. *Let's Visit Vietnam.* London: Burke Publishing, 1983.

Nguyen, Lan. *Vietnamese Folktales.* Hayward, California: Alameda County Superintendent of Schools, 1981.

Vuong, Lynette D. *The Brocaded Slipper and Other Vietnamese Tales.* Reading, Massachusetts: Addison-Wesley, 1982.

Index

About the Author

Sherry Garland has been helping Vietnamese families in the Houston, Texas, area since 1981. She has many Vietnamese friends and frequently attends festivals and family celebrations.

"Hopefully, this book will promote better understanding of the Vietnamese culture among American schoolchildren," she writes, "as well as teach Vietnamese children aspects of their history, culture, and homeland, and create a sense of pride in their heritage."

A free-lance writer and a member of the Society of Children's Book Writers, Ms. Garland received degrees in French, English, and linguistics from the University of Texas at Arlington. She has published two novels for adults and a young adult novel. Currently, she is working on a collection of Vietnamese fairy tales and a novel about an Amerasian girl in Vietnam.